I AM THAT I AM

Doneta —

As is written on p. 100
The Kingdom of God, the Kingdom of Heaven
is love, light, life
and oneness with the I AM.

and on p. 53
Dwell ... Abide ...
in the secret place of the
Most High.
It is the grace of the I AM
that allows you to show forth
peace, wholeness, health
immortality, oneness.

May we continue our spiritual growth
as we share in experiencing that Oneness.
Love Always. — Betty

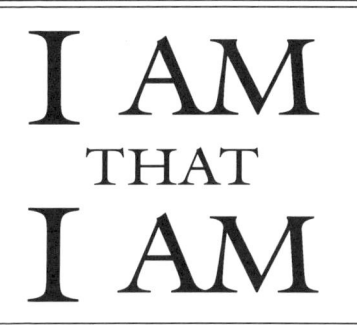

*E*xperience the nature
of your True Self

PAMELA FREEMAN STANTON

I AM THAT I AM

Copyright © 1994 by Pamela Freeman Stanton
First Printing, August, 1994

For information contact:
Stancom Productions
4401 Leatherwood Drive
Virginia Beach, Virginia 23462
804 499-3432 Phone/Fax

All Rights Reserved.
No part of this book may be used or reproduced in any manner
whatsoever without the permission in writing from the author.

Manufactured in the United States of America
Library of Congress 94-092247

ISBN 0-9642797-1-1

Spirit, Mind, Soul and Body

in oneness

with the I AM

Table of Contents

I.	I AM Love	14
II.	I AM Peace	27
III.	I AM Truth	38
IV.	I AM A Consuming Fire	58
V.	I AM Strength and Power	75
VI.	I AM King of Kings	87
VII.	I AM Life	103
VIII.	I AM THAT I AM	124

Foreword

On January 28, 1988, I experienced a dream in which the Father told me I was to write a book, and entitle it I AM THAT I AM. Then I heard an audible voice speak these words three times: "I AM walking over you! I AM walking over you! I AM walking over you!"

I awoke and reached for my pad and pencil from the night stand and the following writing came forth:

Enter now into the Kingdom of God. Hear My Voice. Because of your openness in seeking truth, and your faithfulness and love, the I AM is walking over you.

The Spirit of God is walking over your carnal soul, mind, will, emotions, and body. Listen. . .You are One with the I AM. Your redeemed Soul is joined together with Spirit, becoming One with the I AM, One with the Father. This is the true marriage. I designed it this way before the foundations of the world. You are a New Creation, a New Man. The I AM, the Father of Lights, reveals man's true Self, man's real Identity. Realize and accept that the nature and character of God is your Being. I AM Spirit, I AM Life, and so are You. Always remember, whatever your need is, I AM.

Rejoice and welcome this mystical marriage. With every circumstance, trial, test, experience that comes to you, be at peace and know that the I AM is the only power in the Universe. This hidden wisdom is in God in Christ. It is the I AM that is ruling "all" aspects of your Being. You live and move and have your being in the I AM. No longer see the Adam nature, self-will, the carnal mind, or duality thinking, residing in you. Its place is under your feet. The grace of the Lord Jesus Christ be with you.

Awake to this perfect love of the Father in you. Arise each day in the glorious awareness of the I AM in you as You. Live in the NOW and be transformed and set free this day. You will notice a change, just like the one that happened yesterday when no thought of good or evil came to you, no thought of duality thinking, when you were being persecuted. This is living in Love; this is the river of Life in You; this is union with God.

The I AM in you expresses Itself as God, and that expression comes forth as the Pure You, the Christ You, for We are One! No longer does the "you" of you exist. The I AM is all that IS. I AM walking over you daily setting you free from the beliefs and the bondage of your carnal mind and bringing you into the

Will of the I AM, the fullness of God. It is written, you have the Mind of Christ. Allow the Spirit of Truth, the Holy Spirit, the still, small Voice of divine Intelligence within, the I AM, to lead you into all Truth.

I, the fullness of the Father, am arising and manifesting Myself completely in your Spirit, Mind, Soul, and Body. Where I AM you are, for We are One in this eternal union. All I have is yours. My perfect light, life and love are available to all. Believe and receive your oneness with the I AM. I created you in My image and likeness for you to show forth My glory.

Write and record, as the I AM within you directs. My Presence is always in you. Be the express, visible image of the invisible God now and into eternity. Heavenly, Spiritual, Holy Union with the I AM, the Father, is your life, your existence. Experience and live this Truth. There is One Body, One Spirit, One Faith, One Baptism, One God and Father of all, who is over all and through all and in all. I AM THAT I AM. So Be It.

Pamela Freeman Stanton

I do not pray for these alone,
but also for those who will
believe in Me through their word;
that they all may be one,
as You, Father, are in Me,
and I in You;
that they also may be one in Us,
that the world may believe that
You sent Me.
And the glory which
You gave Me I have given them,
that they may be one
just as We are one;
I in them, and You in Me;
that they may be
made perfect in one,
and that the world may know that
You have sent Me,
and have loved them as You have loved Me.

John 17: 20-23

Preface

This book is designed so you
may read, reflect, and meditate
on any one chapter,
page, or statement.

Permit the I AM to lead you into all Truth.
The goal, the purpose,
is to experience the FATHER.
Realize and live this oneness.

GOD IS . . .

All are called to perfection,
to eternal joy,
to Holy Union in the Father.

I AM
Love

**I AM THE MOST HIGH GOD.
I AM THE RULER OF THE UNIVERSE.
I AM THE FAITHFUL GOD
WHO LOVES ALL.**

I AM THE MOST HIGH GOD . . .
Full of love and mercy!

I love you with an undying love.
A love that is everlasting.
A love that is infinite,
measureless, endless.

A love that is continuous,
full of glorious joy.
An eternal love without
beginning or end.

There never has been a time
I have not loved you,
had compassion for you,
or forgiven you.
I chose you in the I AM
before the creation of the world.

Rejoice and be glad!

Neither death, nor life, nor angels,
nor principalities, nor powers,
nor things present, nor things to come,
nor height, nor depth,
nor any created thing shall be able to
separate you from My love which
is in Christ Jesus.

The I AM is the Spirit of Eternal Love.
I AM in everyone.
Your redeemed Mind, Soul, and Body
are open to this divine
inflow of perfect love.
With boldness, enter and experience
your oneness with the I AM.

Perfect love is the Christ You, the Spirit You.
The life-giving, creative Force,
the Holy Spirit,
the Spirit of the Father
is your Spirit Self,
for We are One Spirit.

The I AM circumcises, cleanses,
renews, and transforms your heart,
beliefs, emotions, and mind.
I AM love.
This perfect love heals past
or present memories that bring you pain,

grief, worry, and strife.
All these feelings and thoughts are
coming out of your self-will,
your emotions of the flesh
that leave you unconscious of truth.

Day by day I pour out
My steadfast love upon you.
The I AM leads you into
the bosom of God.
I AM the fountain of living water.
Be refreshed.
Be restored.
Thirst no more.

Your Spirit Self, your Christ Self,
is the Incarnation of the love of God.
The I AM within you gives
love, light, and life to
your whole Being,
to your Mind, Soul, and Body.

Submit to God within.
Experience divine stillness.
Partake of the intimate, inward oneness
of the I AM.

Be clothed with pure virtues,
with a robe of innocence,
with perfect love and humility.

This is truth . . .
Your redeemed Soul, your Consciousness,
your Subconsciousness, your Mind
and your Body
are not alienated from the
I AM,
your Spirit Self.

I, Christ Jesus, have rolled away the
darkness of sense thoughts,
of self-will.
I paved the way for a permanent

ascent into the Most Holy Place,
the Spirit of God within.

I cast all sin, all rejection of God,
all evil, weakness,
disease, lust, greed, pride
into the fire of
perfect love.

I redeemed your earthly, temporal, worldly
mind, soul, and body
and brought you into
oneness with the I AM.
Therefore, love, esteem, and worship
the I AM, the Most High God,
with all your Heart, Soul,
Mind, and Strength.

Love mercy
and have compassion for all.
Understand and accept

the love of Christ
which surpasses all knowledge.
This love is the fullness
of the I AM.

Give, impart to all,
this most prized possession,
this most prized gift . . .
the eternal love of the I AM, the Father.

There is only one Source of love.
It is the I AM,
the Most High God of Everlasting Love.
Abide in this infinite love.
Be sure of it. Rejoice in it.
Experience a joy, a gladness, a conquering
of all things as you walk in oneness
with the I AM.

It is through the Spirit You,
the Christ You, that eternal love binds

up and heals wounds, dissolves error,
and restores light and truth.
This takes place in the invisible,
as well as the visible realms.

Remember . . .
every Soul, every Person, every Creature,
is your neighbor.
The I AM loves all the kingdoms
of the world . . .
heaven above, earth, and under the earth.
Apply merciful, healing love to all.
Encourage, comfort, and in every way, love
and preserve any form in which
there is life.

Let go of all desires and beliefs
that are separate
from the I AM, the Spirit of God.
These cravings are coming from the ego,
from the Adamic or carnal nature.

This need for self-will and self-effort
is all a delusion, a lie, and has no truth.

This is the reality . . .
This is the truth . . .

The I AM has dethroned
all self-life, all human nature.
It is dead!
The I AM imparted the divine,
eternal Christ life in all so that
all may live by Spirit.

Return within to the Spirit You
and obey the I AM,
the God of Everlasting Love.
The old, painful beliefs in duality
will be replaced with the I AM,
the Christ You.
Your True Self in Spirit union with
the I AM expresses only one nature . . .

the nature of the Most High God.

All I have is yours.
My perfect light, life, and love
are available to all.

Your resurrected Soul and Body
are filled with this flawless life,
peace, love, joy, compassion, and mercy.
Be willing to be open to this truth.
Your redeemed Soul and Body are the
consciousness and manifestation of God.

You are free from condemnation,
free from the curse of the law,
free from sickness and disease.

All of you . . .
Spirit, Mind, Soul, Body
is in oneness with the I AM,
the Father.

Divine love brings you into
the righteousness of the I AM.
Divine love restores all back into God.
Divine love forgives, is gentle, patient,
kind, faithful, and courageous.
Divine love gives you a Resurrected Life
in Christ that is perfect and eternal.
Divine love sees God's life in all.
Divine love is the I AM that I AM
in fullness.

The I AM in you as You loves all
creation with a pure heart.
The I AM loves in deed and in truth.
The I AM respects all men.
The I AM is the Mind of Christ
and so are You.
Experience peace on earth,
peace in your Mind, Soul, and Body,
as you send out love, goodwill and blessings
to every man.

Have boldness.
As the Indwelling Christ, the I AM,
is perfect love, so are You.
Hold fast to the Pattern of infinite love,
which is Christ in You.
Your nature is the nature of God.
Your thoughts are the thoughts of God.
Your memory in Spirit remembers only oneness
and union with the Father.

The I AM is the Ruler of the Universe.
I rule over all forces within your Being
and over all energy in the universe.
I have always ruled. I always will.
I AM God and Father of all.
I AM over all and through all and in all.

LOVE and MERCY is My name.
LOVE and MERCY is Your name.
You are One with the I AM,
One with the Most High God of Love.

THIS IS ETERNAL LIFE!
THIS IS UNION!
THIS IS ONENESS!

I AM
Peace

**I AM THE ALMIGHTY GOD.
I AM THE EVERLASTING FATHER.
I AM THE SPIRIT OF TRUTH.
I AM THE PRINCE OF PEACE.**

I Give Peace.
That Passes all Understanding.
BE PERFECT,
BE OF ONE MIND,
LIVE IN PEACE
AND
LOVE ONE ANOTHER.

I AM peace.
Look not on the outside of you
to find this peace,
nor look within your ego,
your carnal mind,
your worldly soul,
nor your earthly body to find peace.

Do not look for an individual to give
you peace, nor think that
changing jobs will bring you peace.

Moving to another location
will not give peace.
More money will not bring peace,
nor will the healing of
your body bring peace.

I could go on and on with excuses
and defenses that the
self-willed man thinks will bring peace.

Remember . . .
the world will never give peace.
The I AM has overcome the world.
Listen to the I AM
within the Spirit You
and live in peace, in safety.
I give peace to all.
Receive the Spirit
of power, love, and a sound mind.
Be open to truth
and your heart will not be troubled or
be afraid of anything.

I AM ALL AND IN ALL.
Be at peace.

Perfect peace I give you.
I, Christ Jesus, have broken down
the middle wall of partition
between Us . . .
the wall between your carnal soul,

your beliefs in duality,
and the Spirit of the Father.
I have made Us One.

Rejoice . . .
for the Light has come!
Be thankful.

Peace is the Real You.
I, the Almighty God, give you strength
and bless you with truth, understanding,
wisdom, and counsel.

Believe and experience all your
thoughts at rest and at peace.
Complete . . .
One with the I AM.

Feel the creative, pure thoughts
of the I AM within your whole Being.
These perfect ideas burst into a melodious

song that produces harmony, agreement,
unity, and oneness in all things.

The I AM, Christ, has told you many
times that those things which you
have heard and seen Me do . . . DO!

I, the Indwelling Christ, am the
glorious Light of the Father.
I bring peace from heaven,
from the divine realm of Spirit,
from the I AM,
into your carnal,
physical, earthly, temporal
mind, soul and body,
forming a Redeemed You.

Peace is your nature.
Peace heals the nations.
Peace solves the questions you
are asking right this moment and

gives you understanding.
Peace clothes you with light
and sets your worldly mind, will, emotions,
and body free.
Free to be who you really are . . .
the eternal, life expression of the I AM.

The I AM releases the hurts that
live in your human mind and soul.
This untruth within the
self-centered you keeps you from
expressing life.
I give truth
that transforms the falsehood,
the lie, the misrepresentation
in your whole Being.
I make you free.

Let go!

The union, the marriage, of God's Will

with your human will, with your carnal soul,
with you earthly body,
has taken place.
Welcome and experience the
Presence of the I AM within all of you.

Be silent . . . Be quiet . . .
I AM Spirit and so are You,
for We are One.
Listen to the Spirit You,
the still, small voice of God within.

I shall be within you wisdom,
righteousness, peace, and joy.

I AM that burning Light within that is
always radiant, shining, blazing with love.
I bring truth, encouragement, and support
to set your imagined self free.

I AM in all of you.

I AM your Consciousness,
I AM your Intellect, your Mind,
your Soul, your Senses, your Body.
Welcome the peace that
passes and transcends all understanding.
Never will I leave you.
Never will I forsake you.

This perfect nature of love and peace
consumes any confusion or disapproving beliefs.
I, the Spirit of Truth,
bring you into LIFE,
into the fullness of the Father.

Be still . . . know . . . I AM GOD.

Before Abraham was, I AM.
The I AM, the Christ, is ready to arise
in your carnal mind, soul, and body.
I have paid the price to set you free.
I appear as soon as you are

ready for the Christ to emerge,
even sooner than
you are ready.

I come quickly!
Return to the Spirit You
and experience peace and life.

The marriage, the union,
of the Christ Spirit
and the soul of humanity
has taken place,
thus becoming One.

The inner nature of pure Spirit is
now your outer nature.
You have entered into Christ
who is peace, becoming:

One with joy,
One with love,

One with truth,
One with wisdom,
One with patience,
One with the Universe,
One with the Father.

Belief in limitation and separation is gone.

Self-gratification is gone.

The curse, the effects from eating of the
knowledge of the tree
of knowing good and evil,
is gone.

The self-will is gone.

Perfect peace and harmony is manifested.

Spiritual love is the normal state and
condition of your Being.

The living Spirit of God, the I AM,
your Spirit Self, your Christ Self,
expresses life in all creation.

THIS IS THE GOAL.
THIS IS THE FULFILLMENT.
THIS IS THE PURPOSE OF YOUR BEING.
THIS IS THE GRACE, THE UNMERITED FAVOR,
OF THE I AM FOR ALL.

I AM
Truth

I AM THE LIVING, ETERNAL GOD.
I AM THE SPIRIT OF TRUTH.
I AM THE SPIRIT OF THE FATHER.
I AM THE SPIRIT OF CHRIST.
I AM THE HOLY SPIRIT.

Allow the Spirit of Truth,
the still, small voice of
divine Intelligence within,
the I AM in you,
to lead you into all truth.
Follow this inner voice of truth.

The Spirit You, the Christ You,
will always do
what pleases the Father.

The I AM is your Christ Self,
for We are One.
This redeemed Inner You expresses only
the nature and character
of the I AM, the Father.
You are as I AM. You are Spirit.

The Spirit of Christ,
the Holy Spirit, has come.
The I AM teaches your worldly soul,
your self-will, your beliefs
that are separate from the I AM,
the reality of the full knowledge, wisdom,
and understanding of where you came from
and who you are.

I have instructed you to be

in the world, but not of it.
This truth that the I AM speaks
brings corrective judgment to you,
to all persons
and
to all nations.

I AM the Creator.
I AM the Word of God.
The I AM lives within you as
the Christ You, the Spirit You.
I AM the way, the truth,
and the life.

I AM all and in all.

I, Christ Jesus,
bring you into all truth.
I deliver you into the Father.

TRUTH makes you free . . .

Free from the bondage of your earthly soul,
your unsurrendered mind, will, and emotions.

Free from the reasoning of your intellect.

Free from your self-will.

Free from your ego.

Free from the belief of separateness of your
life from the life of God.

Free to be the divine, eternal
expression of the I AM
now and into all the dimensions
of creation.

The Christ within is the whole law,
both the inner and the outer law.
Stand still.
Look within to the Spirit You.

Listen to the voice of truth.
The Holy Spirit
within your inner Being
becomes the teacher,
and you will no longer need to be
taught by the outer law.

The outer law is God's law.
Its purpose is to reveal and expose
the slave relationship
to self-will, to self-delusion,
and to invite you to look
within to the Spirit You.

Believe and receive your oneness
with the I AM.
I created you in My image
and likeness for you to
show forth My glory.
Your true desire is to obey
the inner leading of the Spirit You

and experience LIFE.

Truth has crucified self-will.
Choose the will of the Father within
and fulfill the complete law of God.
The Indwelling Christ is the Spirit You,
the Real You, the Pure You.

I AM love and so are You,
for We are One in this Holy Union.
Self-will, carnal mind, rejection of God,
sin, death, Satan
cannot exist in this union
between You and the I AM.

Open yourself fully to the
entrance of truth.
The Holy Spirit appears and
transforms your unsurrendered, human
thoughts, beliefs, convictions,
doctrine, and religion.

Trust the I AM.

I give sight to those who are
spiritually blind,
and I show those who think they see
that they are blind.

I, the Eternal Spirit,
the Spirit of Life,
bring you into an experience
and knowledge of your
oneness with the I AM,
the Infinite God, the Father of all.

Truth is . . .

There is no opposite in the I AM.
Understand this reality.
Enter into the Most Holy Place,
the Father, where the I AM,
the Spirit You, lives.

In truth, the I AM, the eternal God,
is the only Spirit, the only power,
the only strength in the universe,
the heavens, the cosmos.

Awake! Arise!
The redeemed You is One with the I AM.
The I AM is one God.
The I AM is Father of all.
The I AM is over all, through all,
and in all.

The I AM is your Spirit,
Mind, Soul, and Body.

It is written:

Everyone who asks, receives.
Everyone who seeks, finds.
Everyone who knocks,
finds the door opened.

Simply,
That which you ask for, I AM.
That which you seek, I AM.
That which you knock at, I AM.

Desire and choose truth.
Submit wholly and entirely to God.
Always seek to find the
final confirmation of truth
for yourself
from the I AM within you
as the Christ You.

Be receptive.
Be alert.

Watch the presence of God
within the Spirit You
as you open
your consciousness
to the Infinite Christ,

to the Mind of Christ Jesus,
to the Father.

Permit the I AM
to be manifest, to be visible,
to reign in your Soul,
in your individual life and affairs,
in your attitudes, mind,
will, and emotions.

Live not by might, nor by power,
but by the Spirit of the
Living God.
This realization
brings the Kingdom of God,
the consciousness of God,
on earth.
This is the I AM living
in you as You.
I AM the inner anointing that
teaches you all truth.

At this moment, I appear within you
as glorious Light.
This Light is the fullness of the Father,
the Son, and the Holy Spirit.

Be wise.
Let truth, let God
enlighten you.

The I AM is Christ, the Beloved Son,
the only Begotten Son.
I AM THAT I AM.
I AM in you and you are in Me.
We are One.
All I have is Yours.
All My ways are just and perfect.
I AM the Source of Eternal Salvation.
I AM the Lamb of God.
I AM the Word of God.
I AM Truth.
I AM the Father.

Receive and experience
this truth,
this oneness!

I AM the Maker of heaven and earth,
the sea and all that are in them.
All live within you.

Heaven is the I AM Eternal Spirit . . .
The Spirit of the Father, the Spirit of Christ,
the Holy Spirit, within you as You.

Earth is the manifestation of the
I AM God Consciousness . . .
The outer truth expressed through
your Redeemed Soul and Body.

The sea is the I AM Mind of God . . .
thoughts and ideas
within the Spirit You, that are
All-powerful,

All-knowing,
All-present.

The I AM is in all humanity, and
all humanity is in You,
for the whole world is but one family in
the I AM.

You shall know the truth,
and the truth shall make you free.
Rejoice always in truth.
Be full of compassion. Be merciful,
gracious, long-suffering, and kind.
I AM the life in you that cannot die.
I AM the vision that motivates
and empowers you.

The I AM creates you,
forms you, and establishes you to be
a visible manifestation
of the invisible God on earth.

Awake.
Arise and walk in light.
Understand that the Spirit of Truth,
the Power of the Highest,
is guiding you, protecting and
leading you always.
Sing a new song,
the beautiful Eternal now,
which is oneness with the I AM now!
Experience life given to all parts
of your Being.

This new song is a melody of love,
a melody filled with harmony and joy.
It is a song worshiping the presence of
the I AM Eternal God within all
your Being.

The I AM is God, the Indwelling Christ,
in you as You in this Holy Union.
Welcome this mystical marriage

of your Soul and Spirit
to the Indwelling Christ.

Demonstrate your oneness
with the I AM
by opening your carnal mind,
your consciousness, to truth.
Abide, remain, continue
in this spiritual truth
which is limitless.
Divine love within you is selfless
and free from fear.

This perfect love is manifest
in the joy of giving.
As you are One with the I AM,
you are One
with this perfect love.
Recognize . . . acknowledge . . .
and greet the Christ in every man
and in every living thing.

Receive the truth
that there is no separation
between the good and the bad,
between the religious and the secular,
between the sinner and the saint.

Heavenly, spiritual, holy union with
the I AM is your life . . . your existence.
Worshiping the Father in Spirit and in
truth is your desire.
Always doing the Will of God,
inwardly and outwardly,
is your will.

Dwell . . . Abide . . .
in the secret place of the
Most High.
It is the grace of the I AM
that allows you to show forth
peace, wholeness, health,
immortality, oneness.

Acknowledge God.
Be responsive, be sensitive,
to the Spirit of Truth
within you.

The I AM,
the fullness of God,
appears within you and expresses
Itself as God,
and that expression emerges as the
Pure You, the Christ You.
The purpose is to praise, honor,
worship and reverence the Father.

Listen.

It is the Spirit, the I AM,
within that reveals
and declares the glory,
majesty and light of God,
and the redeemed Soul shows forth

and demonstrates
the nature, likeness, and image
of the I AM.

The I AM proclaims and enlightens
you as to your Christ Self
through Paul when he wrote:
I have been crucified with Christ.
It is no longer I who live,
but Christ lives in me;
and the life which I now live in the flesh
I live by faith in the Son of God
who loved me and gave Himself for me.

Know the truth.
GOD IS!

All truth about God
is the truth for every individual Man,
for God and Man
are One.

Therefore,
You are the church of the Living God,
the pillar and ground of truth.

You have a purified Soul,
full of God consciousness,
full of light and power.

Your Body is the temple of the Living God.

You need not any man teach you
for you are One with the I AM,
the Father,
Son, and Holy Spirit.

You are an individual,
the unique and perfect expression
of the eternal I AM,
the Most High God.

I AM Spirit and so are You.

I AM Truth and so are You.
I AM Grace and so are You.
I AM Peace and so are You.
I AM Love and so are You.
I AM Life and so are You.

Press toward this end.
This is your purpose for being,
to realize and experience this oneness.

Welcome, believe, accept
and live truth, the Word of Life,
in this life as well
as the life to come.
Walk in love, walk in light,
walk in unity, walk in wisdom.

ALL ARE CALLED TO PERFECTION,
TO ETERNAL JOY,
TO HOLY UNION
IN THE FATHER.

I AM
A Consuming Fire

I AM GOD.
I AM A CONSUMING FIRE.
I AM LIGHT.
I AM LOVE.
I AM PURE.

I AM a consuming fire.
I AM divine energy
that never ceases to give life,
to dispense love,
to impart pure thoughts,
to declare truth, to grant power,
to provide intelligence.

The I AM accomplishes My purpose
through the divine fire of love.
These pure thoughts of the
I AM within you
cleanse, purify,
purge, temper and transform
your carnal mind,
your earthly soul and body
into perfect light,
into life,
into love.

Remember . . .
I AM light.
My nature produces pure thoughts.
Be receptive.
Receive the Mind of Christ.
Open your entire Being to the
inflow of Christ.

Yield totally to having your

secret thoughts and intents
transformed by truth,
by the I AM.

I AM pure.
I see you as pure,
for We are One.

I AM Spirit and so are You.
I make my abode
in heaven which is within
the Spirit You.
This is the residence
where the I AM tabernacles.
Worship the I AM
in Spirit and Truth.
Encounter a divine relationship
with the Father.

Listen . . .
The wisdom that you hear

is first of all pure,
then it is peace loving,
considerate, submissive,
full of mercy and good fruit,
impartial and sincere.

Return to the Father.
Stand in the Holy Place
within the Spirit You and accept
your True Identity, your oneness
with the I AM.

I, the Spirit of Truth,
the Holy Spirit,
see your pure heart.
I direct you
into the channel of love,
into Christ, who is spotless,
unblemished, unmixed,
blameless, innocent, genuine,
perfect.

The I AM sees you as complete.
Stand firm in this truth.

Lack of faith and sin
occur only when the carnal,
temporal soul of man listens
to the flesh nature,
the Adam man.

Have confidence.
Listen only to the Spirit of God
within you, your Christ Self.

The I AM sees no evil.
My eyes are too pure,
too full of love,
too full of kindness,
to look on evil.

The battles that you experience
are not in your Spirit.

These untruths
are in your unsurrendered soul,
your ego, the beliefs in the Adam man,
the carnal mind
that is refusing to
accept your Real Identity,
your Divine Self,
your Spirit Self,
which is One with the I AM.

The I AM,
the Light of the Spirit within you,
corrects and changes
attitudes, opinions,
priorities, rebellion,
stubbornness, misunderstandings,
bad feelings toward others,
shameful remarks from your lips
into the Image and
the Likeness of the I AM,
your Real Nature, your Divine Self.

The I AM calls you into life.
Enter into the I AM
and experience this oneness.
Be released
and be the fullness of the I AM.

Be willing
to believe the truth.
Be willing
to accept the marriage
and the union
of the human soul of man
to the I AM,
to the Spirit of God.

Welcome this union with all creation
and experience abundant life.

Allow this oneness
with the I AM
to swallow up the lies,

the false teachings and beliefs,
you have chosen to believe.

The I AM,
the Father,
appeared in Jesus Christ
to destroy untruth in all humanity
once and for all.

It is finished!

Release negative thoughts,
false teachings of your family,
friends, school, religion,
community, and the world.
Feelings of shame and low self-esteem,
being belittled for feeling angry,
sexual desires and actions,
being afraid to be who
you really are in God
have all been

purified and cleansed
forever
by the Fire and Life
of God through Christ Jesus.

The accuser within your earthly soul,
self-will, the Devil,
is defeated and
forced out of power
by Christ Jesus.
It is written . . .
I, Christ Jesus, live wholly
in you, for We are One.

Be conscious
of this oneness between
You and the I AM.
Hear the Word of God,
the I AM,
declaring into your whole Being
the truth of oneness.

Be strong and vigorous in truth.
Be free.
Reside in life.
Live in complete harmony
with each other.
Allow your life to overflow
with joy and thanksgiving.

The I AM has redeemed you.
You are a New Creation,
a New Man,
filled with the life of God.
It is the I AM
that rules all aspects of your Being.
The I AM is the fullness
of the Godhead.

Experience harmony, oneness
and union with the Father.
I AM the Lamb of God.
I have no desire to inflict pain.

I have redeemed you
and have given you life.

Embrace the Presence of the I AM,
the life of Christ,
within you wholly . . .
Spirit, Mind, Soul, and Body.

In so doing,
you will not be tormented
with negative thoughts,
with untruth.

Refusing to accept
your Real Identity,
your Christ Self,
is what causes strife,
separation from the truth,
sickness, disorder,
lack of love, lack of peace,
and lack of joy.

It is written:
You cannot serve two masters.
Be willing to die,
to crucify any illusion,
any evil desire,
any thought that takes you
away from the Presence
of the I AM within you.

Listen.
The sovereign authority of the I AM
crushes the thoughts
of opposition and resistance
of the earthly soul
and the carnal inventions of man.

The inward quickening
and sustaining life of God
brings all things
into light,
into truth, into peace,

into joy, into love.
It is the purpose of the I AM
to dethrone "self-life"
and to impart the
Christ life
so that all may
live by Spirit.

Meditate on this truth.
I, Christ Jesus,
destroyed all evil,
all error, all stubborn wills,
all flesh, all carnal nature
and converted it all into
heavenly light.

Be the
rich, fertile, creative,
fruitful treasures
of the I AM.
Enter into fullness of life,

into victory,
into glorious liberty,
into love
that transforms all things
that are not
of the Christ nature.

Behold . . .
the tabernacle of God is in Man.
Rejoice.
There shall be no more death.
The I AM wipes away
all tears, all pain, all sorrow.
I make all things new.

Obey and accept
the truth of oneness with the I AM.
Love one another
deeply from the heart.
Abide in the I AM.
Remain in this love where the heart

is blameless,
pure, whole, and complete.

Be perfect
even as I AM perfect.
Yield to the love
of the I AM within you.
Be what I created you to be . . .
the complete, visible manifestation
of the I AM,
the fullness of the Father's
Image, Nature, and Likeness.

Believe this truth.
Accept this truth.
Live this truth.
This awakening, this enlightenment,
is happening
right this moment within you.
Believe. Have faith.
In this Holy Instant,

be set free
from eating of the
knowledge of the
tree of good and evil.

Come.
Enter into silent awareness.
Hear the Voice of the I AM.
Partake and eat
of the tree of life and live.

The I AM
reveals and unveils
the Kingdom of God within you.
You are born again of an
imperishable seed
through the
living and enduring
Word of God.

Be illumined.

Divine completeness
and eternal perfection
in the I AM
is your purpose for Being.

Realize . . .
All that I, the Father, have is
for you, for We are One.
There is no separation
between God and Man,
for God and Man are One.

Receive this truth.

Rejoice in this truth.

Be the presence and
the expression of the Father
now and into eternity.

I AM
Strength and Power

I AM STRENGTH AND POWER.
I AM CHRIST.
I AM THE SPIRIT OF TRUTH.
I AM THE FATHER.

I AM all strength and all power always.
I make your direction,
your way, perfect!

I reign over all with wisdom,
power, and might.
I AM your deliverer, your saviour,
your shelter, your protector,

and your shield.
It is in God that you live and move
and have your being.

Be Still . . .

Listen within the Spirit You
and hear the I AM that is ready and
willing to enlighten you
to your True Self.
You and I are One.

It was the grace of God that brought
this about. Nothing can replace
this truth.

I AM always present within you
for You are My dwelling place
for We are One.
I give breath and life to all.
Be at peace.

Rest in truth.

It is the strength and power
of the I AM
that exists, whether visible
or invisible.
I AM behind all power and strength.

Be open always
to the fullness of truth.
To the degree that you believe
and accept your true inheritance,
your oneness with the I AM,
are you and all creation able to rise
above every trial, affliction,
weakness, and limitation.

The blood of Jesus Christ has redeemed
your carnal beliefs,
your disobedience, and will
to be separate from God.

The I AM, your Christ Self,
is always ready to transform thoughts
that live within you
that are alienated from the Father.
It is written,
You and I are One.

Choose the I AM as your shelter
and strength.
In so doing,
the thought of death
within you will loose its power.
You will enter the secret
dwelling place
of the Most High God.

The I AM is waiting
for you to let go of self-will.
Permit the Holy Spirit, the Spirit of Truth,
to bring you into the Will of the Father,
into joy, peace, and life.

The I AM is above every man,
thought, and desire.
Be calm.
Be at rest.
Abide in this circle of Love that is
continuous, full of glorious joy.
Arise from lifeless, dead beliefs and thoughts
and awake in the Resurrected Christ,
the Resurrected You.

The I AM is your refuge
and fortress.
I, Christ Jesus,
have conquered all worldly
thoughts and rebellious urges in you
to be a separate self from the I AM.

Divine love rescues,
releases, and frees your human mind,
earthly soul and body
and brings you into

the Mind of Christ,
into life,
into love,
into the Father.

Accept your oneness with the I AM.
Harm and disaster will bypass you.
I have given you a Spirit of power,
love, and a sound mind.
I encircle you with songs of deliverance.
The Christ You has conquered
all fear in all of you.
You have entered into trust with
the Most High God, the Father.

I have girded you
with strength and power.
The inner voice of the I AM,
the Spirit of Truth,
will guide and direct your thoughts.
I give you understanding, knowledge,

discernment, and sensitivity.
I tell you what actions to take
and when to take them.

Rejoice, for the I AM will not
let you slip.
I watch over your life.
I never slumber or sleep.
I keep you from all harm if you will
but listen . . .
listen to that still, calm voice
within the
Spirit You which is the I AM.

The grace, the unmerited favor,
of the I AM
is enough for all.
You and I are One, no longer two!
The redeemed You
is created with the
nature and life of God.

Believe . . .
have faith and know that power,
strength, salvation,
and the Kingdom of God has come
within all of You.

The accuser within your earthly mind
is overcome, cast down.
The belief in duality
no longer exists
between You and the I AM.

Trust the I AM.
I always succeed.

I AM truth.
Truth makes you free
to know your True Self,
your Christ Self.
I bring exalted ideas,
divine aspirations,

and pure motives to this Union
between Us.
I AM endless life and power.
Welcome your oneness with the I AM.
Enter a New Life filled with ever increasing
strength and power.

I AM faithful.
I, Christ Jesus, am your Pattern to follow.
I conquered self-will.
So shall you,
for You and I are One.
No man can pluck you out of the I AM.

I have given you eternal,
ageless life.
The Christ You, the Real You, is life.
Nothing can separate you
from this eternal love.

Accept and experience this mystery

which is Christ in You.
Victory is won in the I AM.
The I AM is the Spirit
of the Living God
that lives within you
as your Christ Self,
your Spirit Self.
We are One in this Holy Union.

Have confidence and boldness.
You and all people have access by faith
into this Spiritual union of oneness
with the Father.

Your carnal, earthly
mind, will, and emotions
go astray when you desire
to follow your self-will,
instead of the Will of the I AM,
your Heavenly Father.
You repent and ask for forgiveness

because you have not come to the
complete realization of your
oneness with the I AM,
with the Father.

Know the scriptures and the strength
and power of the I AM.
The Father created you to be a unique,
visible expression of the I AM.
Have confidence
and trust only in your Christ Self,
your Spirit Self.

Surrender totally to the truth
of the I AM.

You are in the I AM
and the I AM is in You.

The I AM is your life,
your strength, your power.

You are One Spirit with
the I AM.

Christ is all in You.

You are a perfect, unique
and visible expression of
the I AM,
for You and I are One!

I AM
King of Kings

I AM KING OF KINGS.
I AM LORD OF LORDS.
I AM THE FATHER.

The I AM, Christ Jesus, is
KING of Kings and LORD of Lords.
The place of My throne is within
the Son of Man where I live.
I reign with enduring strength,
power and glory.

The nature, the character, the temperament

of the I AM is your Christ Self,
for You and I are One.

The I AM is supreme over all.
Every knee, every carnal thought,
shall bow, yield and submit
to the KING of Kings,
to the Christ Spirit.
Every tongue, every spoken word,
every religion
shall confess Jesus Christ is Lord.
I AM all and in all.

The I AM will shine through
your human eyes
in beauty and brilliance
for the very Light of Life
stands behind them.

Truth brings life
into your whole Being

so the perfect image of the Father
may be expressed.

Harken to and obey the voice of
the Holy Spirit,
the voice of wisdom,
truth, and love.
The Son of God, Son of Man,
ascends and sets your earthly
soul and body free.

This perfect expression of God,
the Spirit You, the Christ You,
destroys all human senses,
the kings within your rebellious
mind, soul, and body,
conscious or subconscious,
in the purifying fire of Spirit.
Understand and accept that
the Real You, the Christ You,
is One with the eternal I AM.

As you embrace this truth,
the belief in duality will decrease.
The I AM, the Christ You, will increase.

I AM the Light within you that
spotlights the carnal forces ruling
in the soul of man.
I bring these fleshly kings,
all human senses,
into Spiritual perfection.

The true desire of these temporal
kings that rule within the
mortal, imperfect
soul and body
is to bow down, obey,
and worship
the I AM, the KING of Kings.

These worldly kings can be identified
by their natures . . .

The self-willed intellect
seeking to gratify self;

the rebellious urges to be a separate
self from the I AM;

desiring temporal, materialistic
things instead of eternal;

lustful sexual desires and practices;

the belief that strength and power
are physical instead of Spiritual;

the human belief that death is
unconquerable;

the worship of false gods;

and the mind that clings to man-made
creeds, organizations, or to

religious leaders.
Very simply . . . all self-will,
all outer confusion, sense confusion,
and mental confusion, shall obey the
I AM, the Father of all.

Choosing earth-bound thinking, self-will,
leaves you unconscious of truth.
This hinders and delays these
kings in their desire to surrender to
the I AM, the Indwelling Christ,
the Spirit You.

Be open and welcome your New Life in Christ.
Your Real Self in Spirit union
with the I AM represents only one nature . . .
the nature of the Eternal God.

All powerful thought forms in the
conscious and unconscious mind of
humanity have been purified

and cleansed
by the Christ Spirit,
the Spirit of Love.
These thought forms
include self-delusion, self-will,
evil influences and desires.

To the degree that you open
yourself and accept your oneness
with the I AM, with the Father,
do you live in life, in harmony,
in peace, in love.

The I AM is Victorious and Glorious.
I AM Enduring Strength and Stability.
I AM the Spirit of Truth
that balances the
negative and positive forces
bringing about
wholeness, completeness, and soundness.
I AM the Enlightening Power

that brings Salvation.
I AM Righteous Rule
and Righteous Judgment.
I AM Peace and Perfection.
I AM Overcoming Power.
I AM Perfect Love.
I AM Life.

The I AM has released You
from the genetic coding,
rules, and standards
of your family and ancestors.
I, Christ Jesus, have delivered you
and brought you into oneness with the I AM.
You and I are One
in Spirit, Mind, Soul, and Body.
Believe and experience this truth,
this holy union.

Everything in man shall recognize and
acknowledge its source, its oneness,

in the I AM, the Almighty God.
Say to each turbulent thought:
Be still . . . know . . . I AM GOD.
By faith accept this truth wholly
in all of you.

Return to Spirit.
As the I AM is Christ,
so is the Real You.
It is no longer
the flesh man that lives,
but it is
Christ that lives in you as You.

The Holy Spirit is ever present.
I, the Spirit of Truth,
seek to reveal
the total fullness, union,
and oneness of God in Man.
Christ Jesus has established a New Man.
This redeemed Son

is created to be the unique
expression of perfect love.
Your Christ Self wants to worship,
honor, respect, and glorify
the Father in Spirit and truth.
Receive and welcome the truth
that you are wholly indwelt
by the Spirit of the Father.

Boldly accept that
the Father is in You
and You are in the Father.

This acceptance is true worship,
for in true worship
only God and the redeemed Soul of man
are necessary.
There is only
one God and Father of all.
The Christ You is perfect
and desires to express

the Life of God in
all dimensions of your Being.
The I AM is at work in you
to accomplish
all that I desire.
I AM standing open, unveiled,
unrestricted before a purified
and cleansed Whole Man.

Be transformed
into Life, into the Kingdom of God.
You are the Son of Man and the Son of God.
The I AM will have you travel
beyond the limits of man.
I call you Faithful and True,
for Faith and Truth, Soul and Spirit,
have united as One.

Your True Identity, your Real Self is . . .
One with Christ.
One with Truth.

One with Faith.
One with the Word.
One with the Son of Man.
One with the Son of God.
One with the Father.

It is only when you know yourself as
the Christ Self
do you experience
oneness with the Father.
Your purpose is to recognize and be
this inner nature and uniqueness of God.

Within this New Man, which is Christ,
the Name is written:

KING of Kings
and LORD of Lords.
The redeemed You, the Christ You,
is in total balance
between the human you and the divine you.

No duality exists.
A melody of love and harmony flourishes
as you experience
oneness with the Father.

The I AM is Ruler and Master over all
faculties of the Mind.
I rule over all the thoughts
that are guided by the senses.
I AM over every created part
and aspect of your Being.
I AM over all things . . .
in heaven, in earth,
underneath the earth,
on the sea, and all things in them.

I AM the Most High God.
What I perform,
what I create
is perfect.
What I decide, what I judge

is done in perfect love
with a perfect outcome.
I bring you out of immature
thinking into the freedom to
accept and be your True Identity,
your Christ Self.

Arise!

Be the fullness of the I AM.
Let go of self-will, duality thinking,
and freely accept
your oneness with the Father's will.

The Kingdom of God, the Kingdom of Heaven,
is love, light, life
and oneness with the I AM.
Righteousness, peace, and joy abound
when you welcome
wholly in You the I AM.
Oneness with the Father is the reality.

Listen . . .

You cannot on your own strength
awaken the I AM God consciousness
within yourself.

You can, however, by faith
receive the marriage and the union
of the human soul
to the Christ Spirit,
to the I AM, to the Spirit of God,
and thereby
become a visible manifestation of the
invisible God on earth.

To the degree that you are open
to the truth of oneness
with the I AM,
which includes a life
that is immeasurable,
limitless, immortal, eternal,

endless, unchanging, timeless,
everlasting, and infinite
do you take on the character,
nature, and powers of God.

This Spiritual union between Us
accommodates
one will, the Will of the Father.
I AM the Vine and You are the Branches.
I AM the Living Water
and You are the Container
that houses the I AM.
I AM the same yesterday, today, and forever.

I AM ALL and in ALL,
the ETERNAL GOD!

I AM
Life

**I AM SPIRIT.
I AM THE MOST HIGH GOD.
I AM THE FATHER.**

I AM life.
In the I AM there is no death.
I AM eternal,
indestructible, imperishable.
Life always is; life always will be;
life never has not been.
Listen carefully and hear the voice
of the I AM within you.
I AM the Spirit of life,

your Father-Mother God.
I AM light, love, and life.

Everything that exists in heaven
and earth shall find its perfection and
fulfillment in the I AM,
the Spirit of the Living God,
your Real Nature,
your Divine Self, your True Self,
the Life of God.

In the beginning,
you were sent out of the I AM
as Light, as Intelligence,
as pure Spirit.
I AM Spirit
and so are You.

My image is male and female
together in
One Spirit, One Mind,

One Soul, One Body.
I have never walked
out of your presence.
I AM everywhere.
There is no time
or space in the I AM.

The I AM is the Spirit of God.
I created you in My image.

Hear this truth . . .

It is My life, My breath,
that is breathed into your nostrils.

You and I have always been
united in Spirit.
Never to be separated,
never to be divided.
There is no duality in the I AM,
the Most High God.

Turn inward.
Return to Spirit in the inner
chamber of your Being
and discover the glorious
Light of Life, the Most High God.
You and I are One.
Embrace and never let go of this truth,
this reality.
This truth will liberate you.
This truth will make you free.

I AM life. I AM immortal.
I AM eternal. I AM infinite.

I AM the fountain of life
that abides in the Spirit You.
Life always flows from
within your Being
to be manifested out.
It is the Father within you
that shows you the path of life.

This life is full of joy and pleasures
for evermore.

I AM in you
expressing and declaring
Myself not only
in you but
through you,
for We are One.

I move and have My Being in you.
You are my offspring,
My beloved Son,
in whom I am well pleased.
Everything comes out of the I AM.

I AM omnipotent,
all powerful.

I AM omnipresent,
ever present.

I AM omniscient,
all knowing.

Where I AM, you are,
for We are One.
I will never leave you
or forsake you.
The I AM will always comfort you
and give you peace.
I AM with you always.

I AM Spirit.
Harken and hear My Voice of truth.
Life is spiritual.

Your physical body may change and take
another form, but life endures,
life continues.
There is no ending,
for every end, every termination,
every conclusion,

is a new beginning, a new start,
a new experience
into a greater life in the I AM.

Be still . . .
Know I AM God.
Fix your eyes not on what is seen,
but on what is unseen.
I have told you what is seen
is temporary,
but
what is unseen
is eternal.

You came out of the I AM,
the Father-Mother God.
You are a chosen generation,
a royal priesthood, a peculiar people.
I see Myself in you,
only life.
This celestial, divine seed

of the I AM in you
lives forever.
Nothing can destroy this life force.

I AM the resurrection and the life.
Peace and love
are manifested in your entire Being.
I clothe you
with heavenly clothing
not made by man,
but made only by
the Most High God.

Enter this divine,
eternal temple within you,
the dwelling place of the Father,
and experience life.

Open wide your heart.
Be filled with My mercy, love,
peace, and joy.

Thoughts in your mind, will,
and emotions
that are mortal, temporal, deadly,
imperfect
are swallowed up by life,
by truth, by the Father.
You are in Christ,
and Christ is in the Father.

Arise.
Receive the gift, the promised seed,
from the Father.
Become One Body, One Spirit,
One Faith.
I AM over all, through all,
and in all.

I AM the source and origin of life.
I AM the tree of life.
I AM that pure,
crystal river of life.

Because I, Christ, live,
you also shall live.

All authority
in heaven and earth is Mine.
As the Father has life in Himself,
so has He given to the Son
to have life in Himself.
I, Christ Jesus,
lead you into the bosom of the Father.

Drink of the pure water
that I give you,
and you shall never
thirst.

I AM heavenly love.
I AM the shining glory of the
Father awakening pure thoughts
in your Mind.
Choose life.

Open the window of your heart
to the I AM, to God in Christ,
the Eternal Light.

All that is necessary
for life thoughts to emerge
is an inner longing and spiritual desire
to drink of the water of life freely.

Awake!

Accept your oneness with the I AM.
Commune directly with the Father.
This river of life,
the living Spirit of God,
flows from within
bringing
life, love, peace,
and harmony
to the earthly soul of man
and to humanity.

Experience the marriage and union
of the human soul of man
to the Christ Spirit, to the I AM.
You and I are One.

The I AM, the Lord God,
arises from His holy temple
within the Spirit You.
Live and declare the truth of oneness.
I AM in you to be represented forth
to all creation.
Take heed to the Real You,
the Spirit You, and live.
I AM your Being.

Christ Jesus came from the Father,
from Spirit,
to redeem you
from the Adam consciousness.
You no longer have the
consciousness of the old man,

the beliefs in duality.
You are a New Creation,
a New Man,
created in the likeness
of the I AM.

Be conscious
that I AM your life.
Your testimony, your redeemed Soul,
will confess this truth,
for I, Christ Jesus,
have made Us One.

I came to bring you into the
Father.
Rejoice and be glad.
The I AM is the overflowing
fountain within you that is
always ready to give
and communicate
My nature to you.

Hear truth . . .
God and Man are One.
Perfect harmony exists between US.
Death has been swallowed up
in victory through Christ Jesus.
I destroyed death,
and brought the good news of
life everlasting to all.

Awake.
Be refreshed.

Return to Spirit and walk
in the statutes of life.
Display the virtues
and perfection of the I AM
who called you out of darkness
into His marvelous light.
Live and be this expression.
Experience a total dependence on the
Spirit of God within your whole Being.

The will of the Adam man
no longer chooses.
It is the will of the Father
that is desired.

It is in the I AM
that you live and move
and have your being.

Remember . . .
Think about such things as
whatever is true, whatever is noble,
whatever is right, whatever is pure,
whatever is lovely,
whatever is admirable,
whatever is excellent or praise worthy.

Whatever you do,
do all things to the
glory of God.
By love serve one another.

Because Christ lives,
all shall live.

I AM Spirit
and so are You,
for We are One.
In nothing be ashamed.
With boldness
allow Christ to be magnified,
to be glorified,
in you wholly.

As the I AM, the Father, has life,
so have I given life to You,
My Son.

Have a wholesome tongue,
hold fast to the instructions
of the I AM.
Accept and experience
your oneness with the I AM.

Be crowned with loving kindness
and tender mercies.
I show you the path of life.
I bring fullness of joy.
Believe and live life.
I AM infinite fullness.
Behold the beauty of the I AM.

Hear the GOOD NEWS.

I AM appearing now!
I AM appearing in truth,
in joy, in love.
Allow the Presence
of the I AM
to be manifested,
to be unveiled,
to be proclaimed
out of the Real You,
the Spirit You,
into your whole Being.

Now is the time to see
and experience Life.
The old man, the Adam man,
has been crucified.
The New Creation Man is all there is.
It is finished!

Know God in your heart,
rather than by outward forms.
The presence of the I AM
brings you
into the consciousness,
realization, and awareness
of the I AM.
Accept your True Identity.

I AM the bread of life.
Come into Me and never hunger.
Drink of My truth within and
never thirst.
Be spiritually minded

and experience life
and peace.

Know the truth of
your Divine Self, your Spirit Self.
Be free.
The old man, the Adam man,
the belief in duality,
wants proof that
You and the I AM are One.

Listen to My Voice . . .
The New Man, the Redeemed Man,
the Christ Man, the Corporate Man,
the Spirit You,
has no need
to prove your True Identity.
Recognize no man
according to the flesh.
Living in the Spirit
is your reality.

Doing the Will of the Father
is your desire.
Believe,
accept, and represent
the I AM
in your Spirit, Mind, Soul and Body.

Your purpose for being is
to reveal God's Glory and Light.
Live in peace, live in joy,
live in love.

THIS IS UNION BETWEEN
GOD AND MAN.

THIS IS THE MARRIAGE OF THE
SOUL OF MAN
TO THE SPIRIT OF GOD.

THIS IS SONSHIP.

THIS IS ONENESS.

THIS IS LIFE.

THIS IS THE GLORY OF
THE FATHER.

I AM
THAT
I AM

I AM THAT I AM.
I AM THE LORD GOD.
I AM THE MYSTERIES OF CHRIST.
I AM THE SON OF GOD.
I AM THE SON OF MAN.
I AM THE SPIRIT OF TRUTH.
I AM THE FATHER.

It is written: I AM full power
and authority in you.
I AM light, I AM the source
of eternal salvation,
I AM everlasting love,

I AM the Word of God. I AM the way,
the truth, and the life.
I AM merciful,
I AM the bread and the water,
I AM the Mind of Christ.
I AM a consuming fire,
I AM the creator, I AM wisdom,
I AM love.
I AM the Son of the Father,
I AM THAT I AM.

Hear MY Voice!

Whatever your need is, I AM.
Be open. Believe.
Have faith, confidence, and trust.

Permit the Spirit of Truth,
the Nature and Character of God,
the Holy Spirit, the I AM within you to
lead you into all truth.

Where I AM, you are, for We are One.

This is reality . . .

This is truth . . .

I AM in you and you are in Me,
for We are One in this eternal union.
I AM the presence of God,
the Indwelling Christ,
in you as You.
I, Christ Jesus, am the way to union
with the Father.

Awake . . . arise to this
realization, this undivided unity,
this complete oneness in your whole Being.
Experience the full measure and joy
of knowing that I, Christ Jesus,
am in you and you are in Me,
and We are in the Father.

There is one God and Father of all
who is over all and through all and in all.
All came from the I AM Almighty God
who is the only presence, power,
and strength within you.
In the Father all abide
and to Him all return.

The I AM is the Father.
Listen to the Spirit of Truth,
the Holy Spirit, within you.
Faith to enter the fullness of the Father
comes only by accepting the truth.
Christ Jesus is in you as You.

There is but one Lord Jesus Christ
through whom you live,
move, and have your being.
All creation is seated with the Father,
for I, Christ Jesus,
have received you unto Myself.

This truth, this blessing is right
now while upon earth.
The I AM is inside you in the
realm of Spirit.

This realm is unlimited
and full of glorious love.

I invite you to experience this marriage
between you and Me.
I AM in you and you are in Me.
Complete unity!

Welcome your oneness with the I AM,
with Christ Jesus,
with the Father.
This Light within you is perfect love.
Perceive and experience that
it is I, the Father, who is
living in you to accomplish My Will.
The I AM is Christ.

I came to bring you back into oneness
with the Father.
I AM the way,
the truth, and the life.
The goal, the purpose, is to
experience the Father!

No longer do I call you to just accept
the grace, the unmerited favor of
the I AM.
I call you to be a giver,
a fountain of everlasting life,
the nature of the Father
in the Son.
The I AM brings you to a place
where you are like the Father
in every manner, deed, act,
gesture, and way.

I AM the Lord God and there shall
be no other gods before Me.

To the measure that you are open
and believe are you changed
into a glorified appearance.

The I AM, the Christ You,
transforms you from mere flesh man
into the express, visible image of the
nature and character of the
invisible God.

I AM pure Spirit, I AM endless life,
I AM infinite intelligence,
I AM love.

You are alive with Christ Jesus
because of My love, mercy, and grace for you.
I brought life to you even when you
were dead in transgressions.

The genealogy within you contained thought
forms of self-delusion, self-will,

desires, and urges to be separate
from the I AM.

It is written:

You are dead.

Your self-life, your self-will,
your belief in good and evil
is dead.

Your New Life is hidden with Christ in God.
The New Man within is Christ!
The I AM releases, delivers, and frees
you from all genetic coding of your
family and ancestors.
I bring you into an unlimited realm.

Accept and experience
this illumination within you
of perfect love.

Jesus Christ crucified on the cross
the self-life of all humanity,
the false god Satan.
The unconscious mind composed
of destructive mental patterns,
rejection of God,
and all fleshly senses
is overcome.
The grace of God through Christ Jesus
tasted death for every man.

I, Christ Jesus, gave Myself
as a ransom
for all.

The I AM made a Blood Covenant
with you and all of humanity
that continues forever.
I created a Redeemed Son, a New Man,
based upon a perfect
Spirit, Mind, Soul, and Body.

I, Christ Jesus, arose from the dead
by the glory of the I AM,
the Father within Me.
You also arose from the dead,
for You and I are One.
You are reconciled, reunited with the Father.

It is finished!

Life and oneness in the I AM
is your inheritance.
No one can snatch you out of
the Father's hand,
for You and I are One.
The I AM is your identity.
I AM in you as You.
I AM your life.

The Devil,
the shinning, most powerful angel,
self-will,

is banished from heaven by God.
Heaven is the Spirit You.

The accuser within your soul, self-will,
is defeated, conquered, and overthrown
by Christ Jesus.
My purpose for coming to earth was to
take you and all humanity
back into the Father.

The I AM sets you free from being
unconscious of truth.
I bring you into eternal, endless,
everlasting life.
It is written that I, Christ,
live wholly in you,
for We are One.

I AM in you as the Real You,
the Resurrected You, the Christ You.
In the I AM, all is possible.

You are perfect in character and in nature.
Be conscious, have knowledge,
and experience within you this glorious
oneness between You and the I AM.

Be open.

Release the negative thoughts of duality
and come into the Most Holy Place,
the Father's House in you,
the Spirit without measure.
You and I are One.
You came out of the I AM, the Father,
and now you are coming back into the
I AM as I planned.

Everyone's real home is in the Father.
As you enter oneness
with the Father within you,
you recognize immediately that this is
where you have been longing to go.

This is your original state . . .
and will always be.

I AM wooing you and calling you
into this place of My temple within you.
This dwelling place is eternal,
immortal, the only God.
You did not earn the right to tabernacle
with the I AM.
It is My love for you and all creation
that allows you to see
and experience your oneness in the I AM.

I AM the everlasting God,
the Creator.
I form the light
and I create darkness.
I create all, and all I create is good.
The I AM is the author
and finisher of your faith.
I AM your vision.

I AM your teacher.
I AM perfect.

It is not enough for the I AM
to give you the outer truth for you
to experience abundant life.
You, being Spirit,
must come within
to experience the fullness of God.
The I AM yearns to give you
the revelation
and experience of this inner union
with the Father.

To know your Christ Self, you must
have a single vision focused only
on the I AM within.
Do not divert to other people,
to your own fleshly weaknesses,
to partaking of the knowledge
of the tree of good and evil.

Instead, welcome the entrance of truth
in your inner consciousness,
your inner man.

The I AM, the Holy Spirit,
is your teacher.
This inner longing,
this spiritual desire,
to experience truth within
is all that is necessary for the
I AM to flow into your thoughts and Being.

The I AM makes everything beautiful
in its own time.
Eternity is set in your heart
and in the hearts of all men.
The Spirit of Truth desires
to reveal deep and hidden mysteries to
those who love the Father.
Awake to this perfect love
of the Father in you.

Let go of beliefs that keep you
in prison and separate you
from the I AM.

Hear the Word of God, the I AM
speaking in you as You
into your whole Being.
Listen . . . and you will hear
the I AM springing forth as
a river of life in you
directing your every thought,
your every step,
your purpose in life.
This is the true marriage.
This is the oneness with the I AM
that you have been searching and desiring
for so long.

This is Life!
You have been born of water,
Life of God.

You have been born of the Spirit,
Divine Mind and Power of
the Father.

Enter now into the Kingdom of God
within you.
Experience harmony, oneness,
and union with the Father.

I AM the mystery of God,
and of the Christ, and of the Father.
This hidden wisdom which the I AM
ordained before the beginning
of the world
is hidden in God in Christ.
It is the I AM that
is ruling all aspects
of your Being.

This is the great secret of all truth . . .
The I AM and Man are One!

The I AM That I AM,
the power and the glory,
protects you always.
I AM the fullness of the Godhead
and the Source of all.

It is written:

I AM the Father.
I AM the Eternal God.
I AM Christ.
I AM the Holy Spirit.
I AM the Spirit of Christ.
I AM the Spirit of the Father.
I AM the Son of the Most High.
I AM the Alpha and the Omega.
I AM the Most High God.
I AM THAT I AM.

The I AM will have you
experience the planets.

You will see the other Worlds that are
so much larger than Planet Earth
where you now reside.
See how fast you travel . . .
for it is by pure thought
and you are there.

I AM in you as You.

My Name, the I AM,
is on your forehead.
No longer will you experience
stubbornness in your human mind,
for you have the Mind of Christ.

Whoever is thirsty,
whoever desires life,
come within and abide in the I AM.
In this dwelling place
of the I AM in you,
you are transfigured.

Your raiment, the Christ You,
Spirit, Mind, Soul, and Body,
reflects purity, light, love, and life.

This clothing of the I AM
swallows up all sickness, all darkness,
all limitations in the visible realms
as well as invisible realms.
Anyone who wishes may partake of the
pure thoughts of the I AM
and experience abundant life.

Desire,
receive the marriage
and the union of the human soul to
the I AM,
to the Spirit of God.

Welcome this union with Christ,
with the Father,
becoming One Body and One Spirit,

One Faith, One Baptism,
One God and Father of all,
who is over all and through all
and in all.

Hear truth, see truth, believe truth,
breathe truth, drink truth,
experience truth,
speak truth, live truth.

I AM THAT I AM

STANCOM PRODUCTIONS
ORDER FORM

If you would like to receive additional copies of **I AM THAT I AM**, please fill out this order form and enclose a check or money order payable to:

STANCOM PRODUCTIONS
4401 Leatherwood Drive
Virginia Beach, Virginia 23462
804 499-3432 Phone/Fax

SHIP TO:

Name _____

Address _____

_____

City _____

State _____ Zip _____

Book	Qty.	Unit Price	Total U.S.
I AM THAT I AM		$12.95	$
Va. Residents add 4.5% Sales Tax			$
Shipping & Handling $3.00 Per Book			$
		TOTAL	$